Anonymous

The battle off Worthing

Why the Invaders never got to Dorking

Anonymous

The battle off Worthing
Why the Invaders never got to Dorking

ISBN/EAN: 9783337038908

Printed in Europe, USA, Canada, Australia, Japan

Cover: Foto ©ninafisch / pixelio.de

More available books at **www.hansebooks.com**

THE BATTLE OFF WORTHING;

WHY THE INVADERS NEVER GOT TO DORKING.

A Prophecy.

BY

A CAPTAIN OF THE ROYAL NAVY.

LONDON:
THE LONDON LITERARY SOCIETY,
376, STRAND.

1887.

The Battle off Worthing;

Why the Invaders never got to Dorking.

Yes! it is certainly more than an *every year* New Year's Day when we step from the Nineteenth into the Twentieth century, as we shall do at twelve o'clock to-night. A notch seems to be cut out in Time when a century is finished, particularly one so marked with peculiar and much-vaunted characteristics as the Nineteenth. It is not only a year, but a century, that we shall bury to-night. This thought sends my memory wandering back into the past, particularly as regards our own country, and our narrow escape from annihilation.

I have been indulging my humour by looking over some old newspapers and pamphlets, and amongst the latter I found an article, which was originally published in *Blackwood's Magazine.* I well remember the time of its appearing, the May number of 1871, a few weeks after the conclusion of the war between France and Prussia, and while Paris was still in the possession of the Reds.

It was in every way a remarkable pamphlet. Under the title of "The Battle of Dorking; or, Reminiscences of a Volunteer," it gave a most graphic account of a supposed invasion of England by the Prussians. Though generally condemned as visionary by the Press, a latent feeling of insecurity in the heart of the multitude caused it to have a great run. It was this pamphlet, I verily believe, which first stirred the national pulse. Everybody read it, and everybody spoke of it, for it was soon published in a cheaper form, half-a-crown being rather too much, in the opinion of those who were judges, to expect our islanders to pay for even so golden a warning. You can read the pamphlet yourselves, you can see how ably it is written, how all sensationalism is avoided, what an impression of reality pervades its pages, but the feeling you will not have, which was present in the hearts of many who read it in its day, was the terrible conviction, not only of the complete possibility of such an occurrence, but its great probability. This latent dread was painfully strengthened, in many cases, by the personal experiences of those who, having lately travelled abroad as members of different ambulance corps, or for mere curiosity, had seen for themselves, in every individual of that successful race, the intense sense of superiority, mingled with aggressiveness, which marked the new-born German nationality, flushed as it was by successes that the world's history could not match.

At the conclusion of the well-told tale of England's invasion, I, for one, felt my country to be more than half conquered, when her invasion was even possible. Here lay the real bitterness, we were no longer true to ourselves, and all the grand panegyrics of our national greatness, spoken by poets and historians, rose in my memory like spectres, for they were no longer applicable to the England of that day. To me, looking back, the preservation of our empire seems little short of a miracle. You press me to tell you my personal experiences of the invasion of England, how, in short, the enemy never got to Dorking. I am willing enough to accede, and tell my fireside story on New Year's Eve, of the time when the hearths and homes of England were endangered by folly at home, and foes abroad, since I am able also to tell how those homes were saved, never, I trust, again to be imperilled.

I confess I am thankful enough to be rid of the nineteenth century, so superior as it was considered to any of its eighteen predecessors. It will be marked in the history of our country, by the wise historian, as that century which, while it has in the end added to her glory, during the greater number of its years, enervated and threatened to sap her very existence as a great Power; indeed, England saved herself by breaking with the spirit of the nineteenth, and reviving the more glorious days of bygone centuries. The first fifteen years of the nineteenth century were bloody enough, but in them old England at least played a glorious part. At the conclusion of peace the court of our aged king was crowded with crowned heads, paying homage by their presence to our national greatness. In those days we possessed statesmen, soldiers, and sailors; there was no lack of genius amongst us; our country was safe while she brought forth such sons. We had our faults: we were bigoted and cruel towards the sister island, and had various other blots in our home, and perhaps our foreign, policy, but these were covered by our national prestige. A very different era in our history followed. We fell into a state of self-complacency and apathy towards all but our commercial interest. A dearth of great men was apparent. England seeking to isolate herself from the world no longer produced sons fit to cope with it. Our rulers were men of comparatively small calibre, which would have been evident enough but for the fatal indifference which was upon the nation; lulled by a false security, every step of our policy only added to our degradation and, at the same time, to our self-complacency.

It would take too long to enumerate all the signs which, in the eyes of the few who were filled with salutary fears, foreboded the decay of our country. The most prominent were those to which I have just alluded, namely, the dearth of great men, and the national indifference. We have always been a bragging

Power, but, in olden days, we had something to brag about, while, at the time of which I speak, we had nothing, yet, at no period of our history, were we more self-laudatory, and more egotistically inclined to gloat over our neighbours' misfortunes and shortcomings. We soon became, in consequence, well hated on all sides, nor was this hatred towards us mingled with respect, for, while wilfully blind towards our weakness, we had made it apparent enough to Europe and the world at large. Englishmen abroad began to awaken unpleasantly to the fact that their nationality was no longer the same passport to civility and respect. We did not exactly like this, but still it did not impress us as it ought to have done. We hugged ourselves as we saw how other countries fought and bled, how dynasties were overthrown, how revolution spread on all sides, while old England alone looked on apparently unshaken, supplying arms with great impartiality, and patting revolution on the back everywhere, even in the sister island. We condoned the breaking of treaties we had sworn to uphold, and proclaimed aloud the deadly principle of non-intervention, our foreign policy thus becoming utterly unworthy of our position as a Great Power.

It is true we often gave advice gratis, and the English people subscribed munificently to the funds for the sick and wounded on both sides. Indeed we gave to our own poor with the same munificence or extravagance, squandering unheard of sums on them, without any perceptible improvement being effected by this largess; for the lower classes continued to groan in a state of miserable pauperism, unknown in any other civilized nation, while we had colonies all over the world, with large tracts of land crying for labour to till it. We never understood how to treat our colonies, nor how to use them as outlets for our surplus population, and to make them a real source of strength to the mother country. The spirit of selfishness was the curse of England, and we did our best to disgust our colonies into leaving us, treating them as a father treats an illegitimate child in his anxiety to disown his offspring. If ever any colonial policy was penny-wise and pound-foolish, ours most certainly was so. I am not sure we were more religious or moral than our neighbours. Vice raged like a pestilence in our great cities, and statistics of some rural populations proved that female virtue in the lower classes was rare. Our literature abounded in rationalistic and irreligious works, and theories of the most startling and visionary kind were gravely read and favourably reviewed by our leading journals.

To return to our foreign policy. We certainly no longer held our own in European councils; on several occasions we had to eat very humble pie, but this was, if nasty, at least cheap, and if we were told more or less politely to mind our own business, and our opinions were held to be worthless, in general we were most careful to announce beforehand that we had no intention of backing them. We had little concern with continental affairs, for were we not surrounded by a certain *Silver Streak?*

This suicidal idea of isolation and non-intervention possessed the nation. We did not remember and we would not take to heart the words of that wise old scoundrel, Bacon:—*That in this theatre of life it is reserved only for God and angels to be lookers on.*

In spite of our universal economy we paid a good lump sum for our army and navy; and though our army, when compared to continental armies, was a mere handful, scarcely worth mentioning, our navy had always been a *little* superior to any *one* other in Europe, but, strange to say, we never contemplated the possibility of our having two Powers against us, and finding ourselves without allies. And yet all this time a powerful nation was growing up in the centre of Europe, and we saw her power increase, but no warning was conveyed to us by it. We were blind and deaf, we lived on our tradition, and the remembrance of our past glory seemed to us a sufficient answer to any doubt as to our present safety; we were indeed showing symptoms of decay as a nation, and nothing but the shock we received could have saved us from our downward course.

For years complaints had been rife in naval and military circles, concerning the supply of ordnance and other warlike materials to the army and navy. Public confidence in our ordnance department had, said the leading journal, been very severely shaken, and, looking to-day through files of old newspapers, I saw how freely complaints had found vent, complaints from general officers commanding in presence of the enemy, respecting the inferior quality of the arms and ammunition supplied; complaints from adepts, who considered our torpedo boats too small in size, and unseaworthy, and our gunboats deficient in speed.

Indeed, our guns were bursting all over the world, and some of the most powerful ships in the British navy were, in consequence, placed for the time being *hors de combat.*

It was self-evident, that with so many novel inventions, both in vessels and arms, future warfare must inevitably be regarded in the light of one vast experiment, the result of which defied all ordinary rules of calculation. But this unavoidable risk, which our foe would also run on his side, was augmented a hundred fold on ours by faulty material and construction. Witness the numerous fatal accidents when vessels or arms were put on their trial, a trial which had all the advantage of taking place in time of peace, and not in the presence of an enemy. In fact, at the beginning of the life and death struggle in which we were afterwards engaged, so many failures and miscalculations occurred in our implements of warfare, whether from bad founding, or want of practical knowledge in handling them, that we were driven, more or less, to fall back on what might relatively be called obsolete arms and tactics. Thus to a certain extent justifying a prophecy on which I had often ventured, that, in the event of our ever being engaged in a desperate and unequal war with other European nations, that at least in naval warfare, in spite of torpedoes, long range of guns, &c., we should probably find safety and superiority by engaging, as of old, at close quarters.

It was little wonder that thoughtful and practical men looked forward with the deepest misgiving, and felt that, in case of a great war, Nelson himself could not save us from disaster. In his time our navy was double that of France, and beyond the combined navies of Europe. Added to this, as one evening paper pertinently remarked, "Our Admiralty had a way of taking English ships at what they ought to be, which was decidedly misleading, and in consequence the official returns of English and foreign navies gave quite an erroneous idea as to the relative strength of England and her rivals."

All these sinister rumours recalled unpleasantly the shrieks sent up by our neighbour at like discoveries, but made too late: *Nous sommes trahis! Nous sommes trahis!* For France at the time of her invasion had a magnificent army, thoroughly equipped—on paper—but not in fact.

Severely as I have exposed our weakness and our sins, do not think that I was not, even then, proud of our many good qualities, which were I knew obscured, but not destroyed. No, my eyes fill with tears of pride when I think how nobly we have redeemed our faults, and how gloriously we shook off our fatal apathy, when we awakened to our danger; how we discarded our old foibles and trod them under foot. The hour of national danger was the harbinger of our national regeneration, and by God's blessing we are now the happy and glorious country we once fondly but falsely imagined ourselves to be.

Under the comfortable impression that England was safe and happy behind the *Silver Streak*, with which a kind providence had surrounded this favoured child, even whilst the Franco-German war raged under our very eyes, we took little or no interest in the national defence. I remember some honourable member introducing a motion on this question, during which the house was counted out! I was no great politician, but that small fact made a great impression on me at the time. I felt that a nation so indifferent to its own safety could scarcely escape some disaster.

Peace being concluded, reduction on reduction was the order of the day with us, our M.P.'s were nearly all pledged to this course, and local interests were in their eyes of more importance than public safety. We would not keep a look out for rocks ahead; our rulers were blind, and the country spell-bound. Nationally and individually we trusted to the chapter of accidents, and had to bear the consequences.

Our awakening was rude enough. It was not through the gradual alarm of rumour. While pressed by serious domestic troubles in Ireland, one fine morning all England awoke to learn that a formidable alliance had cast its gauntlet at our feet. The basis of the triple alliance was stated with a simple positiveness that meant mischief. The Eastern question was settled at our expense, while a proposed partitionment of Northern Europe gave Germany the sea-board she had so long coveted, of which France also had her slice.

The event is so recent that a very few words will serve to recall how, shortly before the outbreak of war, the Eastern question had been suddenly re-opened by one of those bursts of spontaneous national feeling, which from time to time defy the calculations of the most experienced diplomatists. This burst of enthusiasm, anti-Russian in sentiment, was the insignificant origin of a war that shook the foundations, not only of Europe, but of the whole civilized world.

I, and probably many others, had frequently indulged in speculating on the possible complications that might arise from old standing sources of discord, and international jealousies, but had any man, one month before the outbreak of war, ventured seriously to forecast the sides on which the Great Powers were actually ranged, he would have been taken for a dreamer. It recalled to my mind an ominous Spanish saying:—*God protect us when Herods and Pilates make friends.* For the most striking feature of the situation was certainly the new departure taken in politics, traditional diplomacy seemed flung to the winds.

It is impossible to describe the indignation which in a few hours set all England in a blaze. No Government could have calmed the indignant voice of the nation, roused as it had not been for many a year. The Mediterranean fleet was at once largely reinforced and sent to the Dardanelles, under the command of one of our royal dukes, while a wild cry of "Arm! arm!" went through the land. The lion awoke, and shaking himself, gazed round to measure his resources with those of the newly revealed foes. The national excitement, and the exigencies of the moment, forced an ultimatum from our Government which was sent to the allied Powers.

Almost simultaneously with the despatch of our note, we received news from America that the Fenians were massing in considerable numbers on the borders of Canada; while several fillibustering expeditions were fitting out, whose rumoured destinations were severally Ireland, and our West Indian islands. Our remonstrance flashed along the wires of the Atlantic cable, and Canada and the West Indies sent over their cry for help. Ten ships, and 15,000 troops were at once despatched to their assistance. The rejection of our ultimatum by the Allied Powers arrived before we had time to realize our situation; the same day tidings reached us that the French and German troops had entered Belgium, the Belgian army retreating on Antwerp.

There was never any question as to our rejoinder, all question of pounds, shillings and pence was cast to the winds, and England joined as one man in the action of the Government, when war was declared against the triple alliance. From the half-hearted allies left to us, we had no hope of adequate assistance. Austria had her own hands full. Italy, Spain, and Scandinavia, hemmed in by our powerful foes, were of little avail to us, neither had we time to concert on means of defence with them. We had a powerful though untried fleet, but not a ship to spare.

Our first move was to send a strong

fleet to the Scheldt; tidings coming to us meanwhile that all our merchantmen in the Elbe, Baltic, and French ports were detained, while troops were massing on the sea-board from Hamburg to Brest, we having fortunately been in time to secure the Scheldt.

The Russian fleet not having sailed for the Mediterranean, had joined that of the Germans; the French Mediterranean fleet had passed Gibraltar, conveying a large fleet of merchant steamers. As our sole remaining squadrons were severally occupied in watching the Russian and German fleets off Heligoland, and the French fleet at Cherbourg, we were unable to intercept them. After this all news ceased; the nation became a prey to most painful anxiety. One thing alone was certain, a descent on our coast was threatened in two or more directions.

My own story begins at this period. I was, as you know, a retired officer of her Majesty's Navy, residing at that time in London. You may easily imagine the keen anxiety I felt to take part in the impending struggle. I went at once to the Admiralty, and put my name down for active employment. There I learnt, to my disgust, that the active list was not yet exhausted, so there was nothing for it but to wait my time.

I wandered down to the "Rag," and read greedily all the news I could gather. Both Houses were to meet that night. By a piece of good fortune I came across a member whom I knew, who took me down to the House with him, and, by his friendly aid, I found myself in the already crowded gallery.

The interest of the assembly did not centre on the able speech of the Premier, though the firmness of its tone, and the occasional flashes of eloquence, elicted some approval.

The speech of the evening was made by the First Lord of the Admiralty. He rose amid cheers, not, however, very hearty ones, and I remember thinking at the time, that the minds of members were probably more full of what we had done, and ought to be able to do, as a naval power, than of confidence in what we should do. The first portion of the speech consisted of a statement of our naval resources, which was far from encouraging. It had been the intention of the Admiralty to build a large number of gunboats, of a most efficient kind. Eight had, in fact, already been built, and ten more laid down; which were not, unfortunately, available in this emergency. Of our ironclad fleet, ten were in the Mediterranean, seven in North America and the West Indies, and five in other parts of the world, thus leaving only twenty-three available for our home defence. These again were sub-divided into two squadrons; one in the North Sea kept watch on the coast of Holland and Germany, from the Scheldt to Heligoland, the Scheldt being our headquarters; the second was the channel fleet, which would defend our south coast and look out for the French fleet.

This force was not so large as could be desired. Some old screw-liners and frigates had already been armed, and were now being manned by the coast guard and naval reserve, to form a second line of defence for the protection of our coasts. Steamers of great speed had been sent in all directions, with orders to keep a vigilant look out for any hostile force, which would enable us to put our land forces in motion towards the threatened spot.

It was evident to all that we were not so strong on our own element as we ought to be. We possessed, it was true, a powerful fleet, but half were absent in various parts of the world, and could not possibly take part in this death struggle. Hoodwinked and deceived by the Russians, we had despatched a fleet to the Dardanelles to cope with a fleet which was almost on our coast. Liners would be knocked to pieces by ironclads, and could not operate at all in shoal water, while few or no gunboats were available. The depression of the House was very palpable, and a slight break in the First Lord's speech which took place at this time made it all the more apparent. No cheers broke on the momentary pause, there was a blank feeling in every breast, in such a crisis something extraordinary was called for, some stroke of genius to impart confidence in the universal alarm.

The First Lord looked round, and I was struck at the time, and have remembered ever since with respect, how he rose to the difficulties of the occasion. He took in the temper of the House, indeed the uneasiness was so evident and general that it made itself known without a word being spoken. He at once alluded to this in terms of sympathy, the situation was very grave, nor could he say with truth that we were properly prepared for the impending struggle. He for one did not wish to shirk his share of the blame, while at the same time he expressed his opinion that it was not more due to individuals than the country at large, which had clamoured for economy, and approved of a dangerous inadequacy of defence. This was, however, no time for Government to recriminate on the country, or the country to recriminate on Government; if England were to be saved it must be by speedy action, and by seizing on the weakest point of attack of our threatened invaders, which he believed was laid bare on their passage from their ships to the shore. Here the increased earnestness of the speaker's manner, and the anticipation of some original scheme of defence at once rivetted the attention of the House. He continued:—

"Troops had been known to disembark unopposed, and also when opposed from the shore, but never when attacked at the place of landing by vessels afloat. The panic which must ensue from an active attack of armed gunboats, steam launches, and other small steamers, on crowded boats, flats, or rafts, employed for disembarkation, would effectually stop any such landing, and compel the enemy to retreat."

He compared an armed steamer, drawing little water, when attacking a string of boats full of troops, to a dog-fish amongst a shoal of herrings, or a dolphin in the midst of flying fish.

"Three hundred steam launches could be turned out in a few days; boats with engines would be used to save time, having moveable rifle proof plates to protect the men from musketry, and carrying a gun in the bows, capable of firing shot, shell and grape into the landing forces. Field pieces, howitzers, or even old carronades, would serve the purpose, no delay need therefore occur, as any small engines could be used, and half the number were already in existence. Small steamers, tugs, &c., were being taken up by the Government, to be armed with guns of some sort or other, the larger ones were to be covered with chain cables outside, instead of armour plates. Retired officers of the Navy would be appointed to command these boats, and empowered to raise volunteers along the coast to man them. These three hundred steam launches could be beached anywhere and easily launched in fine weather, and of course no enemy could land or would attempt to do so, unless the sea were smooth. Stationed at a distance of three miles apart, these launches would defend nine hundred miles of coast, while armed tugs and small steamers would be distributed in every harbour or roadstead, and a line of telegraph wires at once erected along the coast to rendezvous the launches, &c., at any given point. Finally a few men-of-war steamers, drawing the least water, would be in readiness, at different ports, to operate against the transports, and complete their discomfiture by running them down."

"It is useless," he went on to say, "to deny that by unforeseen combination, we find ourselves at this moment in imminent danger. We are outnumbered by land and by sea, and have no time to fully utilize our strong natural advantages, but awakened to the full peril of this crisis, and our sense of false security rudely dispelled, let the indomitable spirit of our English nation assert itself, and we may once more defy the world!

" 'Let us be back'd with God and with the seas,
Which He hath given for fence impregnable,
And with their helps, only defend ourselves;
In them, and in ourselves, our safety lies.' "

I shall never forget the ringing cheers which, repeated again and again, followed this speech; the spirit of the House had risen at once on the announcement of this sensible and practicable scheme, and was wound up by the few last words and the apt quotation, to a pitch of enthusiasm equal to their former depression. A gleam of hope, a vision of deliverance was present in every breast.

Next morning a notice was published in the papers to all retired officers to present themselves at the Admirality. I started off at once, put in my papers, and after waiting some hours, received a commission to command steam launch No. 66, ordered at Messrs. ——'s yard, Blackwall, to form one of the 10th Division, South Coast; my own station being between Worthing and Littlehampton.

I was ordered to raise a crew of fifteen men in my district and one engineer, to take them to Woolwich for some slight gunnery instruction on board the flag ship, while I superintended the fitting of my launch, and on its delivery to steam round to my station, haul her up on the beach, and report myself to the commander of the 10th Division at Shoreham, and obey his orders. I hastily packed a small portmanteau, bade farewell to my family, and arrived at Worthing that evening.

No beating up of volunteers was needed, the papers had carried the news, and I found the station crowded with strapping fellows who, seeing my uniform, eagerly offered themselves. I filled up my list, and started off next morning for Woolwich with my men, who set to work at once at the mysteries of gun drill. Good boatsmen they already were, so there was not so much to learn. I obtained the requisite stores, and as my boat was already built, and only required fitting with engines and rifle plates, shipped on the gunwale and removable when not in action, the evening of the third day found us under sail and steam for our station. I had to accept whatever gun I could get, and a 12-lb Howitzer fell to my lot. On our arrival a party of stout fellows hauled us on to the beach. The men pitched a tent we had brought round, and I set the watch, and at once started off for orders.

The instructions given me were plain enough: My boat was to be kept ready for launching at a moment's notice; private signals were given to me, and general directions as to my line of condu in action. The launches were station three miles apart, and in fine weath alternate boats were to be launched, an row, or rather steam, guard, during th night from 10 p.m. till day-light.

I sent off next morning for papers, ar it was very cheering to see how good th public spirit was. Volunteers were flockin to their respective camps, and the whol nation was aroused. The papers mentioned, as a rumour, that the enemy's fleet was moving and our North Sea fleet preparing to engage them.

In the evening, as it was not our guard, I walked down to the station, which was not more than two miles off, in the hope of hearing later news. My way was in sight of the sea all along. I tried to think calmly over the incidents of the last few days. I had been so busy—my mind so employed—that it all seemed like a dream now that I had time to think at all.

The quiet autumnal night, the sweet country air, freshened by the smell of the sea (which I remember was unusally strong at Worthing, on account of the quantity of sea-weed strewn along the shore), soothed my senses, and I felt that I could now view the situation, without the excitement of action, which had possessed me hitherto.

Was it possible, I thought, that this dear land of ours was at this moment in such jeopardy? In danger actually of being overrun by foes, who would sack our homes, and insult our relations? It was too dreadful to think how the heart of all England would be broken by the presence of a victorious and insolent soldiery. I could not realize such horrors, and tried to turn my mind away; but I knew that our fleet was out-numbered, and that, in these days of steam and armour, our once formidable superiority in seamanship would be of small avail. An action would be decided by superior weight and numbers, and a German or French sailor was almost as good a man behind his iron screen as a British Tar.

As to our Army, supposing a landing were effected? I believed our troops of the line to be the best in the world, but the Militia had little drill or discipline, and the Volunteers?—Well, no doubt they would fight like men, but only a few months previously a review had been held, in which about 20,000 Volunteers took part, and the report of the General in command was given shortly afterwards. His words came with painful clearness to my memory, "Notwithstanding a very simple field day, there were grave errors in the positions taken up; and had it been in actual warfare, whole brigades would have been utterly annihilated in a few minutes." This was the force which might shortly be opposed to veteran troops; these officers in command, who could not take up a position correctly, to the most precise and educated soldiers

Europe had ever seen! My ruminations were not cheering; I could only shake them off by a fervent, "God forbid that an enemy should ever land!"

Now that I was engaged on it, it seemed to me incredible that this simple line of coast defence should never have been originated before; it was so English not to have contemplated the idea of striking a man until his coat was off, and he was quite ready for you to come on.

Why, indeed, had we not made better preparations, while now we were compelled to make shift with a scratch lot of boats? As to light draft armour-plated rams, which would have been most effective, we had none.

While these thoughts were passing through my mind, I took a short cut through some fields, and came across an old farm house and yard; it was very quiet, and presented a somewhat deserted appearance, but the farmer's wife passed frequently in and out of the house as I was approaching, and I saw the old farmer himself standing silently before an empty horse-shed. It was evident enough, as I afterwards learnt from him, that his team had been impressed by the Coast Artillery, in which corps his two sons were also serving. He was well satisfied that he and his were able to aid in the defence of the land, but I remember the pensive look of the old fellow, as he stood silently gazing at the empty stalls, before he saw me coming up. The farm lads were all gone, and he and his "missus" were going to remain to look after the pigs and fowls. He did not believe "they Frenchmen would land." The invaders were all the traditional Frenchmen with him. He was eighty-two years old, and remembered when Boney was coming, "but Boney never did come, and it wasn't in reason that they others," with a jerk of his thumb seawards, "would come either." He was a Sussex man, he said, and they could not make him believe that any "footy" Frenchman would ever land on our shore. I told him that I hoped not, quite as heartily as he did, but if they did, he would have time to clear out, and drive his stock away. The old fellow got very indignant at this suggestion. He had an old gun (with a flint lock I believe), into which he intended to put a double charge, to shoot the first Frenchman who came near his house, but budge he would not. With unpleasant reminiscences of the shooting of peasants that had taken place across the Channel, I told him he would most certainly be shot or hanged, but he received my warning with renewed indignation. An Englishman's house was his castle, as all the world knew; no jury would convict him for defending it; that could not be against the law. I walked on, leaving the fine old fellow shaking his head, and muttering to himself. I wondered whether his grey hairs would save his life, should the enemy land, for the old man would certainly have had his shot at the foe, however unsteady his aim might be.

I soon arrived at the station. Telegrams had arrived from Harwich. All yesterday our Fleet had been engaged with the enemy; one German ironclad had been sunk, and another had made for the land, on fire, and evidently sinking. Swift despatch boats were taking the news from the Fleet to Harwich. No Russians had been engaged or seen. The action was off the Texel, farther west than I liked; however, the news was good, and I had a cheery chat with the station-master about it. He promised to let me hear all news at once, as he had engaged several lads to carry messages and telegrams.

I walked back, and found my men smoking their pipes, and preparing to turn in. I told my news, which delighted them all very much. I am afraid we all bragged a good deal about the poor chance any fleet had with ours. I thought the time a good one to get an insight into the character of my men, and so encouraged them to talk, and found much entertainment in their odd sayings. They were nearly all boatmen, or at all events, well accustomed to boat work, and looked upon it as quite natural that "the Queen" (as they put it) should have thought of them as the best defence for the coast. They knew what it was to get a lot of landsmen ashore out of a boat, and quite revelled at the idea of being in among them under these trying circumstances. Being Sussex men, the history of attempted invasions was familiar enough to them; successful invasion was, by the same traditional teaching, an impossibility in their eyes. From childhood they had spelt over the old tablet in the parish church, to the memory of one who, in his day had struck a good blow for old England.

"What time the French sought to have sacked
Sea Foord,
This Pelham did re-pel 'em back aboord."

They were all Pelhams in spirit; a fine, manly set of fellows, rather inclined to be too independent, but I hinted that the least breach of discipline would be visited by simply sending them home. I could soon replace them. This threat was quite sufficient to keep them steady and obedient.

Next morning's papers were full of confidence and congratulations. The country was safe, our Fleet had proved true to its glorious traditions, and although attacked by superior force, had gained a victory which would prove the precursor of many others.

Six ironclads from the Mediterranean fleet were ordered home at once, and five others on the North American station had been relieved by wooden vessels; all these would shortly be home.

The second editions announced that

great confidence had ensued from the news; the funds had gone up to 70 (they had been as low as 55); bells were everywhere ringing merry peals.

The third edition brought news of the Channel Squadron on the coast of France, consisting of ten ironclads and several wooden steam frigates. The main fleet was off Cherbourg; a flying squadron of wooden frigates cruising off Brest. The chief news was the entry of the French fleet from the Mediterranean into Brest. The merchant vessels were convoyed by five ironclads and several wooden men of war. Our flying squadron had made a gallant attack on their rear. One frigate, the *Audacieuse*, and six large merchant steamers had been cut off and captured. Unfortunately we had to destroy our prizes on the advance of some of the enemy's ironclads to the rescue. However, all was very glorious. The frigate, *Undaunted*, had run up alongside the *Audacieuse* of equal force, and, after a heavy hammer-and-tongs pounding for twenty minutes, carried her by boarding. The old English ensign had been hoisted over the tricolour. It was hard to have to set fire to and abandon her.

This news sent the whole country downright mad with joy; it was the old tradition again, the old times of the *Victory* returned. More was thought of this little action than of the far more important one in the North Sea. The other six frigates were also engaged, and had driven off the French rear-guard, but as my men observed, the saucy *Undaunted* had had the *Audacieuse* all to her own cheek, and had knocked "seven bells" out of her.

To add to our sense of security, the glass had been going down for the last few hours, and towards evening a strong blow set in from W. S. W. No guard was kept afloat that night in consequence, as we were quite assured against any attempt to land.

The evening papers announced the theatres open in London, where national songs formed part of the programme, and public buildings were hastily preparing to illuminate.

I do not pretend that I did not share, to a certain extent, in the general elation, but I did not feel comfortable notwithstanding. I could not help feeling that we were over-matched, and that this success might only prove a respite to disaster.

The Germans had fifteen ironclads, the French about twenty-three in the Channel, the Russian Baltic fleet about twelve more, and where were they? Our ironclads numbered twenty-three, of these thirteen were in the North Sea, and ten off Cherbourg. If the crisis could only be staved off until the arrival of others from America and the Mediterranean, eleven sail in all, we might yet do well.

But, alas! our enemies were no fools,

they would make no unnecessary delay; and then,—where were those "infernal Russians"? To me they embodied the secret, and therefore the most dreaded danger.

By next morning the wind and sea had been beaten down by a storm of rain and hail which took place during the night; we had fine weather again, with light air from the eastward. I must tell you that it was the middle of August, and a Saturday, the two engagements mentioned having taking place on Wednesday.

As we could no longer obtain any telegraphic news from the Continent, we were made sensible of the fact that we were surrounded by water, and had drawn up our bridges.

The morning papers brought intelligence that the news of our successes at sea had been received in America, and a good effect produced. The United States government had seized on the fillibustering steamers that were fitting out in the south, and the States Marshal had called on the Fenians to disperse. They replied by crossing the frontier, and were received by the Canadian Militia and one contingent of the line who routed them completely. Without any discipline they soon became a panic-stricken, flying mob.

Success is a wonderful negociator, and America became at once, very civil and sympathetic with the old country, and announced their intention not to press us in our present difficulties. I believe the old feeling of kinship was at the bottom of it, and that they did not like to see the Britisher whipped by anyone but themselves.

Last night Her Majesty had gone to the theatre, and had read out the brief despatch from off Brest, from the royal box, like her grandfather used to do in the old days. After storms of cheering the curtain rose; "God save the Queen" was sung by all the company, followed by "Rule Britannia," and "Britons strike home," the whole audience joining in the choruses. The Prince of Wales had done the same at another theatre, and received a similar ovation. For one brief interval all England was intoxicated, the cup of triumph seemed already at our lips. It was not to last. About dinner-time a messenger arrived from my friend the station-master: "Some bad news had been received, particulars not yet known, fearful depression in town, panic on 'Change; the news was connected with the North Sea."

An hour after we learnt the worst.

The East coast of England was threatened, a junction had been effected between the Russian and German fleets, heavy engagements were taking place, our fleet retreating, fighting, on the Scheldt, attacked from the north and west, and cut off from the Channel. One ironclad had been dismantled, and, with disabled screw, was towed in under cover of other vessels. Transports, supposed to contain the German army, had been sighted standing north, and protected by a lot of gunboats and vessels of war.

Later news told us what a great panic had ensued on the morning's joy and confidence. The Eastern Army Corps had broken up camp, and was marching on the coast. The Prince of Wales had joined his regiment, and was on his way to the coast, the Queen waving them farewell from Buckingham Palace. A sort of grim determination began to settle on everyone. The tug of war was indeed at hand.

A Government report was published in the papers on the progress of our coast defence. All was going on satisfactorily.

Besides the wooden men-of-war, and gun-boats of the Royal Navy, we had now two hundred and fifty steam launches ready and at their posts, a hundred and ten tugs and small steamers were manned, armed and protected with chain cables. They would make very efficient gun-boats, and their number was daily increasing. They were all manned by volunteers, and stationed at the small harbours about the coast; those near the Thames were manned by Thames watermen, who came forward to a man, Trinity pilots being in the larger vessels.

All lights, buoys, &c., were being hastily removed. The Public were exhorted not to despair, the enemy having by no means landed as yet. The East coast had been especially armed, but the Government had not neglected other parts.

I have said that it was Saturday. When evening came, we prepared to launch our boat at high water. The men had made ways of wood, which they had well covered with the plentiful sea-weed; the anchor was laid out, and everything in readiness. The night was fine but misty, and the sea smooth. It would be high water about seven o'clock, and I intended getting afloat at that hour, as it was our turn to take guard, not having been able to do so the previous night in consequence of the rough weather.

Just before launching, our Divisional Commander came round on horseback. I knew him very well, we had been messmates years before; he was a good officer, and a capital fellow. As we shook hands, he told me he had come round to order all the boats to keep afloat during the night as near their station as they could, except the guard boat for the night, which was to steam out seaward, and return to her station at daylight. He told me that vague news had arrived that the enemy was on the East coast, and that some of our gunboats had been engaged with theirs; also, that the French Brest and Cherbourg fleets had joined company, and attacked our Channel squadron with a much superior force. My old friend and I grasped each other's hands at parting, and I remember how the gravity of the occasion wrung, even from our cold English lips, some words of warmth, as we spoke of our dear old country's straits.

I at once ordered my boat to be launched, and the men hauled her out to our anchor; steam was soon got up, the fire having been already lighted. I had stationed my men at their different duties, and exercised them daily at gun drill.

We had nothing in the boat but our ammunition, coal, and two days' provisions. The shot, grape, and schrapnel shell, took up a good deal of room; the iron rifle plates were not yet fixed, they hung outside the boat by lanyards, could be shipped in a minute, and would protect the men from musketry, but not from round shot, shell, or grape.

In smooth water we steamed about eight knots, and with a powerful rudder were able to turn very quickly. We did not offer much mark, and had water-tight compartments to the height of two feet six inches from the keel; for the rest we were an open boat, with a gun in the bows on a slide, and a mast and sail, which we slung outside the gunwale when not in use. Our funnel was low; we were painted grey, with the number 66 in black on the bows.

We steamed slowly out, and it was singular to see the once crowded highway of the world deserted and silent. The lights—green, red, and bright, by which we should have been surrounded in peace time, were now nowhere to be seen. The night wore on, and the men had wrapped themselves in their blankets, and were asleep, except the steersman and look-out.

My thoughts were too much engaged, and too painful, to allow me to feel drowsy for some time, but after I had ordered the engines to be stopped, the stillness, acting on my over-wrought senses, soon sent me off into a snooze. I woke up in a very short time, and found the mist had changed into a thick fog. I went ahead again, to put the boat in the position she must have lost by the tide, and there stopped, the fog being as thick as ever. I soon dropped off again, but my mind was too excited to rest, and I remember dreaming horribly, one of those harassing dreams, where you think that everyone is against you, and that some dreadful catastrophe is impending. I woke up suddenly with the idea that some great monster was panting and breathing close to me; at the same moment, the look-out hailed me in a low voice, and drew my attention to a curious sound. The panting, breathing, throbbing sound of my dream was still in my ears. I was awake, and there was no doubt about it, that coming out of the fog was the sound of steamers—paddles and screws—flap, flap, going easy.

I ordered the engineer to stand by. The sound came on, and seemed all round us. I heard distant voices hailing, but could not make out what was said. I ordered the men to stand to their arms, but to make no noise. The engines were moved slowly to keep way on, and be ready for any action. The vessels were evidently standing in shore.

It might be our own fleet from the Scheldt, or the French fleet from the opposite coast, or the Germans, though not so likely, as they had been heard of on the East coast.

Flap, flap went the screws, the vessels coming on very slowly, and careful not to foul each other. I could, of course, have stood in shore at full speed, and given the alarm, but if these were our own vessels it would be a false alarm. At the same time, I knew that to find out for certain I must get in the middle of them, and had I the right to risk the capture of my boat? As these thoughts passed rapidly through my mind, my course was decided for me, by the dark form of a vessel looming through the fog fifty yards off. I took the helm and stopped the engines, told the engineer to be careful as to noise, and awaited the result, with my nerves strung to the utmost.

The vessel passed without observing us. She appeared to be a gun-boat, and a man in the chains was heaving the lead. Another passed on our other side—we were still unseen. Then we heard the flapping louder and louder; sometimes the steam blowing off, as if a vessel had stopped; sometimes a hail. What language? I could not make out; a general hail is much the same in all tongues.

The fog was too thick to make out much, and I could only see one vessel at a time, and then very indistinctly; every minute or two we had to move ahead to get out of the way. The look-out man reported in a loud whisper, "Ship right a-head!" I gave the word, "Go on easy," and slipped across her bows. I then stopped, determined to have a good look at her. She was a large merchant steamer, but seemed full of men; leads-men were heaving the lead, and orders were given to the helmsman and look-outs. In what language? not English certainly. I listened again, not French, I believed. I almost wished they would hail me, to determine the point. However, she passed on, towing astern some large boats and barges. Just as I had completed her survey, another vessel loomed close to us on the other bow. To avoid her, I had to turn a-head once more; only a few revolutions, and we stopped again. We only just cleared her, and did not escape unperceived, being hailed at once in German. The word was passed aft in a sharp military manner; and again come the hail, this time in very fair English, louder, and accompanied by some order. A rifle was fired at us, followed instantly by a volley. At the first hail, I at once gave the order to go a-head, full speed. I knew our only chance was to make for the shore at all risks, and go past them all; they would not dare to fire in such a fog, for fear of hitting each other, and could not give chase for fear of collisions; besides, it would be very difficult for them to make us out, and they could only communicate by voice. I ordered the men to keep down in the boat, and we pushed on for the land at full speed, being hailed and fired at by three vessels. The leading vessels were only going about three knots, so I passed them as if they had been at anchor. The gun-boat gave chase for a short distance, and fired rifles at us for some time, but were evidently afraid to fire cannon on account of giving the alarm.

We altered course two or three times,

and she soon gave up the pursuit, and lost sight of us. I fancy she was a pioneer, and that her duty prevented her going too far.

It was now getting on for morning, and I calculated that we were about six miles from shore. I felt that I ought to give the alarm at once, and yet I was afraid they might alter course, and felt most anxious to watch them.

We were quite safe from pursuit; the boat had been struck by a dozen bullets, but no harm done.

The weather got clearer, and a light air from the northward began to dissipate the fog, when the look-out reported a boat on the starboard quarter, close to us. She was a steam launch, standing the same way as ourselves, and I concluded she was an enemy's boat in pursuit, and over-hauling us.

I gave the word to prepare for action, ship rifle-plates, and load with grape. I liked the lively manner my orders were complied with, and giving up the helm to an old boatman, whose station it was in action, I stepped forward to see the gun laid for close quarters, and gave orders to hold on our course, to get the enemy as far away as possible, intending to await her attack, and then put the helm over, and let drive at her. However, taking another look at her with my night-glass, I made out the number 64; she belonged to our own division. We secured the gun, bore up, hailed her, and went alongside.

My news was soon told. Her commander agreed to steam in at once and give the alarm, "Enemy standing for Worthing," while I would keep near them and watch their course. We compared notes as to the bearing of Worthing, and away he went with news which would flash like lightening through England, and stir the hearts of thousands to defend their country with their lives.

We eased the engines, and then stopped to look out for the foe.

The light wind from the coast, and the approach of daybreak, had driven the fog seaward; it hung like a heavy pall between us and the coming fleet. We could now see the land, so stepped her mast, and hoisted the danger flag in the hope of its being observed from the shore, towards which we were standing, having the enemy's fleet coming up to us in our rear.

I was soon able to make out their hulls, and should have said, roughly, that there were upwards of a hundred sail, several gun-boats heading them, followed by transports, steam-tugs, and launches, some large men-of-war bringing up the rear.

It was now broad day, and the sun rising out of the hanging mist; the sun which I felt would see one of the most eventful days my country had known; the sun which would set on England victorious, or on England enslaved.

We were soon joined by three other launches; they had heard the news from number 64; our danger flag had also been seen on shore.

Our orders were to give way before a superior force, but to hover about in shoal water, and watch every opportunity to obstruct the landing.

The day was now quite bright, the sun having entirely dispersed the mist, and we could see in the distance the smoke of our flotillas standing up from eastward and westward.

Meanwhile the enemy's gun-boats steamed in shore in two divisions, and formed two lines, facing east and west, thus leaving an open roadway for disembarking the troops.

We could do nothing as yet, their gun-boats had heavy guns, and it was useless to play at long shot with our short howitzers. However, we went round in circles to distract their aim should they fire at us, and awaited our fast coming supports.

In the meantime, the transports convoyed to the space between the lines of their gun-boats; and tugs were soon taking in tow strings of barges and flat bottomed boats, full of troops, and making for the shore.

A few more launches, and one tug with a heavy gun now joined us; thus reinforced, we made for the hostile gun-boats, which at once opened fire on us, though without effect, as we were moving on them. The long line of boats were still going towards the shore. How we longed to break through the gun-boats, and be amongst them, but the fire was too heavy. Our tug was struck several times, and the gun-boats giving chase, drove us back for a while. Much the same was going on the other side of the line of disembarkation, for our boats were also driven back.

We saw the first division land, and had been able to do nothing. The tugs returned for another load, a considerable force being already disembarked. We soon heard firing on shore, and knew that our coast artillery had come up and were engaged.

Our supports were now coming up in

force—armed steamers, as well as launches—and we were soon hotly engaged with the gun-boats on either side. The enemy's large vessels firing distant shots at us, but not daring to come nearer in shore on account of the depth of water. All this time the boats were coming and going between the transports and the shore.

Our steamers, being partially protected by the chain oables, had not suffered very severely, and the launches were so difficult to hit; but I saw one struck by a shot in the bows, which knocked her to pieces. She was close to us, and we steamed up in time to pick up six of her crew, one poor fellow with his arm shattered. A larger steamer had also received an awkward shot, which obliged her to make for the shore as fast as possible.

I am only attempting to describe what I saw on my side, the East attack, fighting, of course, was going on westward of the line of gunboats as well.

Our boats having continued to arrive, we now outnumbered the enemy's gunboats, which began to give way, but their large vessels were feeling their way in, and firing whole broadsides.

Our gallant Commodore now made the signal to the launches to force the line.

In we went, creeping close in shore. We passed the end of the line, and found ourselves among the troop-laden boats and barges.

I cannot describe the whole scene that

now took place, it was too awful. The string of crowded boats swept with shot and shell, the tow cast off, and the drifting, helpless barges sinking with their living freight.

The tugs having cast off the boats, &c., fired volleys of musketry at us, but we had our rifle-proof shields, and did not suffer much.

The most horrible part was, that we went right over sinking boats, and could save no one. It was useless to attempt it. Hands were stretched out for help in vain. We had already six extra men, and four of our own poor fellows were stretched out wounded in the bottom of the boat. It was sickening to see the wild terror as we steamed up to a crowded boat, and drove shot and shell through her. The brave soldiers in her, helpless and unmanned by a form of attack they could not resist, called for quarter.

What could we do? Their own men lined the beach, and, except in some instances where they threw their arms overboard, and hoisted a white flag on a boat-hook, little quarter was possible. Indeed, the slaughter was terrific; all landing was put an end to, for the enemy's gun-boats turned on us, and covered those tugs which were able to tow their barges back to the ships. Our launches then directed their attention to the men who had landed, and by their fire drove them off the beach.

The Commodore now broke through

the enemy's line, and, closing with superior numbers, carried two gunboats by the board.

We had been at work in this way for more than four hours, and the alarm had been given for, at least, seven, when word was passed that our men-of-war from Portsmouth were in sight. The enemy's frigates at once steamed towards them, and were soon hotly engaged.

We were now resting from our labours close in shore, endeavouring to repair our damages, bandaging up the wounds of those who were hit as well as we could, and keeping the enemy off the beach.

Presently the signal went up, "Engage at closest quarters," and that signal was kept flying. We steamed up at once, and, joining the Commodore, drove the gun-boats pell-mell among the transports, which had all weighed and shipped their anchors, and were making for the opposite coast, cutting adrift all their barges and flats.

About this time a round shot struck one of our plates, and shivered it to pieces; an iron splinter struck me sideways on the head, stunning me for the moment; it left me a scar which I have to this day. The old helmsman, who had steered the boat throughout with great skill and coolness, had the top of his head taken off at the same moment. We lost, out of a crew of seventeen men, including myself and an engineer, two killed and five wounded, besides the poor fellow we had picked up with his arm smashed. Our boat had been struck by two round shot and several grape, and was making a good deal of water, although we had plugged the holes as well as we could. The engines had also received some injury, and been stopped for repair. But oh! the elation and joy that we felt. The victory was complete. The enemy were driven back by our fleet, their transports in full flight, without the means of landing anywhere, and, I believe, without the will.

Our loss was very considerable. Seven launches had been sunk, with most of their crew: four armed gun-vessels met the same fate. We had captured five gun-boats and sunk them, and could certainly have afforded more serious loss, for was not our country safe. Every child knows the history of our glorious struggle. How another division of the enemy were beaten off our East coast, after landing about 15,000 men. How a French flotilla never reached our shores, being met by the same flying squadron who had gained the victory off Brest. The forces which succeeded in landing near Harwich and Worthing—15,000 in the first case, and 7,000 in the last—were attacked by superior numbers, and surrendered next day.

On the news of our victory off Worthing, the men-of-war at all the eastern ports put to sea, and captured several transports. The total loss experienced by the enemy was very heavy, at least 50,000 in killed, wounded, and prisoners.

I need not tell you the story of the remainder of the war, how the robbers quarrelled over their continental spoils, and how England, safe from invasion, turned her immense resources to account, and once more became the arbitress of Europe. But it was more permanent important to our national greatness, because we profitted by our lesson, and resolved never more to sink into that slough of false security which had so nearly proved our destruction.

We had no ambition to be a strong aggressive power, but we had learnt that weakness was culpable, because it tempted the strong, and that a great country could not afford to be indifferent to the doings of her neighbours, or refuse to be conscious of her vast responsibilities, while individually we learnt that men must make personal sacrifices for a great object, and that no duty was greater than defence of our native land. As long as the memory of this national shock lasts, England can never be in such peril again, for looking back at our hair-breadth escape, and contemplating, only for one moment, the shame and deep degradation which so nearly overtook us, tears of gratitude rise to my eyes, and my heart glows again to think that the despoiler has not robbed us of our birthright, and that we can still glory in the name of Englishmen.

Listen to the bells, it is midnight! the century is dying! is dead!

Ring out the old, ring in the new,
Ring happy bells across the snow,
The year is going, let him go;
Ring out the false, ring in the true.

THE LONDON LITERARY SOCIETY, 376, STRAND, LONDON.

www.ingramcontent.com/pod-product-compliance
Lightning Source LLC
Chambersburg PA
CBHW032248080426
42735CB00008B/1053
* 9 7 8 3 3 3 7 0 3 8 9 0 8 *